MW01287163

NERF
FIRING TEST RECORD

Version : 1.1.4

Your Photo

This book is _____'s firing test record

Example

BLASTER : *N-Strike Elite Rampage*

TARGET : *bottle*

TECHNIQUE : _____

BULLET : *Standard, blue*

ACCESSORY 1 : _____

ACCESSORY 2 : _____

ACCESSORY 3 : _____

ACCESSORY 4 : _____

ACCESSORY 5 : _____

DISTANCE	1st TEST (10)	2nd TEST (10)	3rd TEST (10)	TOTAL (30)	AVERAGE (10)	ACCURACY (%)
1 M	10	10	10	30	10	100
2 M	9	10	10	29	9.6	96.67
3 M	9	10	8	27	9	90
4 M	7	8	9	24	8	80
5 M	7	7	8	22	7.3	73.33
6 M	7	5	5	17	5.6	56.67
7 M	4	5	3	12	4	40
8 M	2	3	1	6	2	20
9 M	1	1	2	4	1.3	13.33
10 M	1	0	1	2	0.6	6.67
11 M	1	0	0	1	0.3	3.33
15 M	0	0	0	0	0	0

NOTE : *not bad*

BLASTER : _____

TARGET : _____

TECHNIQUE : _____

_____

BULLET : _____

ACCESSORY 1 : _____

ACCESSORY 2 : _____

ACCESSORY 3 : _____

ACCESSORY 4 : _____

ACCESSORY 5 : _____

DISTANCE	1st TEST ( )	2nd TEST ( )	3rd TEST ( )	TOTAL ( )	AVERAGE ( )	ACCURACY (%)
1 M						
2 M						
3 M						
4 M						
5 M						
6 M						
7 M						
8 M						
9 M						
10 M						
____ M						
____ M						

NOTE : _____

_____

BLASTER : _____

TARGET : _____

TECHNIQUE : _____

_____

BULLET : _____

ACCESSORY 1 : _____

ACCESSORY 2 : _____

ACCESSORY 3 : _____

ACCESSORY 4 : _____

ACCESSORY 5 : _____

DISTANCE	1st TEST ( )	2nd TEST ( )	3rd TEST ( )	TOTAL ( )	AVERAGE ( )	ACCURACY (%)
1 M						
2 M						
3 M						
4 M						
5 M						
6 M						
7 M						
8 M						
9 M						
10 M						
_____ M						
_____ M						

NOTE : _____

_____

BLASTER : _____

TARGET : _____

TECHNIQUE : _____

_____

BULLET : _____

ACCESSORY 1 : _____

ACCESSORY 2 : _____

ACCESSORY 3 : _____

ACCESSORY 4 : _____

ACCESSORY 5 : _____

DISTANCE	1st TEST ( )	2nd TEST ( )	3rd TEST ( )	TOTAL ( )	AVERAGE ( )	ACCURACY (%)
1 M						
2 M						
3 M						
4 M						
5 M						
6 M						
7 M						
8 M						
9 M						
10 M						
___ M						
___ M						

NOTE : _____

_____

BLASTER : _____

TARGET : _____

TECHNIQUE : _____

_____

BULLET : _____

ACCESSORY 1 : _____

ACCESSORY 2 : _____

ACCESSORY 3 : _____

ACCESSORY 4 : _____

ACCESSORY 5 : _____

DISTANCE	1st TEST ( )	2nd TEST ( )	3rd TEST ( )	TOTAL ( )	AVERAGE ( )	ACCURACY (%)
1 M						
2 M						
3 M						
4 M						
5 M						
6 M						
7 M						
8 M						
9 M						
10 M						
_____ M						
_____ M						

NOTE : _____

_____

BLASTER : _____

TARGET : _____

TECHNIQUE : _____

_____

BULLET : _____

ACCESSORY 1 : _____

ACCESSORY 2 : _____

ACCESSORY 3 : _____

ACCESSORY 4 : _____

ACCESSORY 5 : _____

DISTANCE	1st TEST ( )	2nd TEST ( )	3rd TEST ( )	TOTAL ( )	AVERAGE ( )	ACCURACY (%)
1 M						
2 M						
3 M						
4 M						
5 M						
6 M						
7 M						
8 M						
9 M						
10 M						
_____ M						
_____ M						

NOTE : _____

_____

BLASTER : _____

TARGET : _____

TECHNIQUE : _____

_____

BULLET : _____

ACCESSORY 1 : _____

ACCESSORY 2 : _____

ACCESSORY 3 : _____

ACCESSORY 4 : _____

ACCESSORY 5 : _____

DISTANCE	1st TEST ( )	2nd TEST ( )	3rd TEST ( )	TOTAL ( )	AVERAGE ( )	ACCURACY (%)
1 M						
2 M						
3 M						
4 M						
5 M						
6 M						
7 M						
8 M						
9 M						
10 M						
___ M						
___ M						

NOTE : _____

_____

BLASTER : _____

TARGET : _____

TECHNIQUE : _____

_____

BULLET : _____

ACCESSORY 1 : _____

ACCESSORY 2 : _____

ACCESSORY 3 : _____

ACCESSORY 4 : _____

ACCESSORY 5 : _____

DISTANCE	1st TEST ( )	2nd TEST ( )	3rd TEST ( )	TOTAL ( )	AVERAGE ( )	ACCURACY (%)
1 M						
2 M						
3 M						
4 M						
5 M						
6 M						
7 M						
8 M						
9 M						
10 M						
___ M						
___ M						

NOTE : _____

_____

BLASTER : _____

TARGET : _____

TECHNIQUE : _____

_____

BULLET : _____

ACCESSORY 1 : _____

ACCESSORY 2 : _____

ACCESSORY 3 : _____

ACCESSORY 4 : _____

ACCESSORY 5 : _____

DISTANCE	1st TEST ( )	2nd TEST ( )	3rd TEST ( )	TOTAL ( )	AVERAGE ( )	ACCURACY (%)
1 M						
2 M						
3 M						
4 M						
5 M						
6 M						
7 M						
8 M						
9 M						
10 M						
_____ M						
_____ M						

NOTE : _____

_____

BLASTER : _____

TARGET : _____

TECHNIQUE : _____

_____

BULLET : _____

ACCESSORY 1 : _____

ACCESSORY 2 : _____

ACCESSORY 3 : _____

ACCESSORY 4 : _____

ACCESSORY 5 : _____

DISTANCE	1st TEST ( )	2nd TEST ( )	3rd TEST ( )	TOTAL ( )	AVERAGE ( )	ACCURACY (%)
1 M						
2 M						
3 M						
4 M						
5 M						
6 M						
7 M						
8 M						
9 M						
10 M						
____ M						
____ M						

NOTE : _____

_____

BLASTER : _____

TARGET : _____

TECHNIQUE : _____

_____

BULLET : _____

ACCESSORY 1 : _____

ACCESSORY 2 : _____

ACCESSORY 3 : _____

ACCESSORY 4 : _____

ACCESSORY 5 : _____

DISTANCE	1st TEST ( )	2nd TEST ( )	3rd TEST ( )	TOTAL ( )	AVERAGE ( )	ACCURACY (%)
1 M						
2 M						
3 M						
4 M						
5 M						
6 M						
7 M						
8 M						
9 M						
10 M						
_____ M						
_____ M						

NOTE : _____

_____

BLASTER : _____

TARGET : _____

TECHNIQUE : _____

_____

BULLET : _____

ACCESSORY 1 : _____

ACCESSORY 2 : _____

ACCESSORY 3 : _____

ACCESSORY 4 : _____

ACCESSORY 5 : _____

DISTANCE	1st TEST ( )	2nd TEST ( )	3rd TEST ( )	TOTAL ( )	AVERAGE ( )	ACCURACY (%)
1 M						
2 M						
3 M						
4 M						
5 M						
6 M						
7 M						
8 M						
9 M						
10 M						
____ M						
____ M						

NOTE : _____

_____

BLASTER : _____

TARGET : _____

TECHNIQUE : _____

_____

BULLET : _____

ACCESSORY 1 : _____

ACCESSORY 2 : _____

ACCESSORY 3 : _____

ACCESSORY 4 : _____

ACCESSORY 5 : _____

DISTANCE	1st TEST ( )	2nd TEST ( )	3rd TEST ( )	TOTAL ( )	AVERAGE (-)	ACCURACY (%)
1 M						
2 M						
3 M						
4 M						
5 M						
6 M						
7 M						
8 M						
9 M						
10 M						
____ M						
____ M						

NOTE : _____

_____

BLASTER : Relon G5-6
TARGET : bottle
TECHNIQUE : aim and line barrel

BULLET : Blue nerf (new)
ACCESSORY 1 :
ACCESSORY 2 :
ACCESSORY 3 :
ACCESSORY 4 :
ACCESSORY 5 :

DISTANCE	1st TEST ( )	2nd TEST ( )	3rd TEST ( )	TOTAL ( )	AVERAGE ( )	ACCURACY (%)
1 M						
2 M						
3 M						
4 M						
5 M						
6 M						
7 M						
8 M						
9 M						
10 M						
___ M						
___ M						

NOTE :

BLASTER : _____

TARGET : _____

TECHNIQUE : _____

_____

BULLET : _____

ACCESSORY 1 : _____

ACCESSORY 2 : _____

ACCESSORY 3 : _____

ACCESSORY 4 : _____

ACCESSORY 5 : _____

DISTANCE	1st TEST ( )	2nd TEST ( )	3rd TEST ( )	TOTAL ( )	AVERAGE ( )	ACCURACY (%)
1 M						
2 M						
3 M						
4 M						
5 M						
6 M						
7 M						
8 M						
9 M						
10 M						
____ M						
____ M						

NOTE : _____

_____

BLASTER : _____

TARGET : _____

TECHNIQUE : _____

_____

BULLET : _____

ACCESSORY 1 : _____

ACCESSORY 2 : _____

ACCESSORY 3 : _____

ACCESSORY 4 : _____

ACCESSORY 5 : _____

DISTANCE	1st TEST ( )	2nd TEST ( )	3rd TEST ( )	TOTAL ( )	AVERAGE ( )	ACCURACY (%)
1 M						
2 M						
3 M						
4 M						
5 M						
6 M						
7 M						
8 M						
9 M						
10 M						
_____ M						
_____ M						

NOTE : _____

_____

BLASTER : _____

TARGET : _____

TECHNIQUE : _____

_____

BULLET : _____

ACCESSORY 1 : _____

ACCESSORY 2 : _____

ACCESSORY 3 : _____

ACCESSORY 4 : _____

ACCESSORY 5 : _____

DISTANCE	1st TEST ( )	2nd TEST ( )	3rd TEST ( )	TOTAL ( )	AVERAGE ( )	ACCURACY (%)
1 M						
2 M						
3 M						
4 M						
5 M						
6 M						
7 M						
8 M						
9 M						
10 M						
_____ M						
_____ M						

NOTE : _____

_____

BLASTER : _____

TARGET : _____

TECHNIQUE : _____

_____

BULLET : _____

ACCESSORY 1 : _____

ACCESSORY 2 : _____

ACCESSORY 3 : _____

ACCESSORY 4 : _____

ACCESSORY 5 : _____

DISTANCE	1st TEST ( )	2nd TEST ( )	3rd TEST ( )	TOTAL ( )	AVERAGE ( )	ACCURACY (%)
1 M						
2 M						
3 M						
4 M						
5 M						
6 M						
7 M						
8 M						
9 M						
10 M						
____ M						
____ M						

NOTE : _____

_____

BLASTER : _____

TARGET : _____

TECHNIQUE : _____

_____

BULLET : _____

ACCESSORY 1 : _____

ACCESSORY 2 : _____

ACCESSORY 3 : _____

ACCESSORY 4 : _____

ACCESSORY 5 : _____

DISTANCE	1st TEST ( )	2nd TEST ( )	3rd TEST ( )	TOTAL ( )	AVERAGE ( )	ACCURACY (%)
1 M						
2 M						
3 M						
4 M						
5 M						
6 M						
7 M						
8 M						
9 M						
10 M						
____ M						
____ M						

NOTE : _____

_____

BLASTER : _____

TARGET : _____

TECHNIQUE : _____

_____

BULLET : _____

ACCESSORY 1 : _____

ACCESSORY 2 : _____

ACCESSORY 3 : _____

ACCESSORY 4 : _____

ACCESSORY 5 : _____

DISTANCE	1st TEST ( )	2nd TEST ( )	3rd TEST ( )	TOTAL ( )	AVERAGE ( )	ACCURACY (%)
1 M						
2 M						
3 M						
4 M						
5 M						
6 M						
7 M						
8 M						
9 M						
10 M						
____ M						
____ M						

NOTE : _____

_____

BLASTER : _____

TARGET : _____

TECHNIQUE : _____

_____

BULLET : _____

ACCESSORY 1 : _____

ACCESSORY 2 : _____

ACCESSORY 3 : _____

ACCESSORY 4 : _____

ACCESSORY 5 : _____

DISTANCE	1st TEST ( )	2nd TEST ( )	3rd TEST ( )	TOTAL ( )	AVERAGE ( )	ACCURACY (%)
1 M						
2 M						
3 M						
4 M						
5 M						
6 M						
7 M						
8 M						
9 M						
10 M						
____ M						
____ M						

NOTE : _____

_____

BLASTER : _____

TARGET : _____

TECHNIQUE : _____

_____

BULLET : _____

ACCESSORY 1 : _____

ACCESSORY 2 : _____

ACCESSORY 3 : _____

ACCESSORY 4 : _____

ACCESSORY 5 : _____

DISTANCE	1st TEST ( )	2nd TEST ( )	3rd TEST ( )	TOTAL ( )	AVERAGE ( )	ACCURACY (%)
1 M						
2 M						
3 M						
4 M						
5 M						
6 M						
7 M						
8 M						
9 M						
10 M						
___ M						
___ M						

NOTE : _____

_____

BLASTER : _____

TARGET : _____

TECHNIQUE : _____

_____

BULLET : _____

ACCESSORY 1 : _____

ACCESSORY 2 : _____

ACCESSORY 3 : _____

ACCESSORY 4 : _____

ACCESSORY 5 : _____

DISTANCE	1st TEST ( )	2nd TEST ( )	3rd TEST ( )	TOTAL ( )	AVERAGE ( )	ACCURACY (%)
1 M						
2 M						
3 M						
4 M						
5 M						
6 M						
7 M						
8 M						
9 M						
10 M						
_____ M						
_____ M						

NOTE : _____

_____

BLASTER : _____

TARGET : _____

TECHNIQUE : _____

_____

BULLET : _____

ACCESSORY 1 : _____

ACCESSORY 2 : _____

ACCESSORY 3 : _____

ACCESSORY 4 : _____

ACCESSORY 5 : _____

DISTANCE	1st TEST ( )	2nd TEST ( )	3rd TEST ( )	TOTAL ( )	AVERAGE ( )	ACCURACY (%)
1 M						
2 M						
3 M						
4 M						
5 M						
6 M						
7 M						
8 M						
9 M						
10 M						
____ M						
____ M						

NOTE : _____

_____

BLASTER : _____

TARGET : _____

TECHNIQUE : _____

_____

BULLET : _____

ACCESSORY 1 : _____

ACCESSORY 2 : _____

ACCESSORY 3 : _____

ACCESSORY 4 : _____

ACCESSORY 5 : _____

DISTANCE	1st TEST ( )	2nd TEST ( )	3rd TEST ( )	TOTAL ( )	AVERAGE ( )	ACCURACY (%)
1 M						
2 M						
3 M						
4 M						
5 M						
6 M						
7 M						
8 M						
9 M						
10 M						
___ M						
___ M						

NOTE : _____

_____

BLASTER : _____

TARGET : _____

TECHNIQUE : _____

_____

BULLET : _____

ACCESSORY 1 : _____

ACCESSORY 2 : _____

ACCESSORY 3 : _____

ACCESSORY 4 : _____

ACCESSORY 5 : _____

DISTANCE	1st TEST ( )	2nd TEST ( )	3rd TEST ( )	TOTAL ( )	AVERAGE ( )	ACCURACY (%)
1 M						
2 M						
3 M						
4 M						
5 M						
6 M						
7 M						
8 M						
9 M						
10 M						
____ M						
____ M						

NOTE : _____

_____

BLASTER : _____

TARGET : _____

TECHNIQUE : _____

_____

BULLET : _____

ACCESSORY 1 : _____

ACCESSORY 2 : _____

ACCESSORY 3 : _____

ACCESSORY 4 : _____

ACCESSORY 5 : _____

DISTANCE	1st TEST ( )	2nd TEST ( )	3rd TEST ( )	TOTAL ( )	AVERAGE ( )	ACCURACY (%)
1 M						
2 M						
3 M						
4 M						
5 M						
6 M						
7 M						
8 M						
9 M						
10 M						
___ M						
___ M						

NOTE : _____

_____

BLASTER : _____

TARGET : _____

TECHNIQUE : _____

_____

BULLET : _____

ACCESSORY 1 : _____

ACCESSORY 2 : _____

ACCESSORY 3 : _____

ACCESSORY 4 : _____

ACCESSORY 5 : _____

DISTANCE	1st TEST ( )	2nd TEST ( )	3rd TEST ( )	TOTAL ( )	AVERAGE ( )	ACCURACY (%)
1 M						
2 M						
3 M						
4 M						
5 M						
6 M						
7 M						
8 M						
9 M						
10 M						
____ M						
____ M						

NOTE : _____

_____

BLASTER : _____

TARGET : _____

TECHNIQUE : _____

_____

BULLET : _____

ACCESSORY 1 : _____

ACCESSORY 2 : _____

ACCESSORY 3 : _____

ACCESSORY 4 : _____

ACCESSORY 5 : _____

DISTANCE	1st TEST ( )	2nd TEST ( )	3rd TEST ( )	TOTAL ( )	AVERAGE ( )	ACCURACY (%)
1 M						
2 M						
3 M						
4 M						
5 M						
6 M						
7 M						
8 M						
9 M						
10 M						
_____ M						
_____ M						

NOTE : _____

_____

BLASTER : _____

TARGET : _____

TECHNIQUE : _____

_____

BULLET : _____

ACCESSORY 1 : _____

ACCESSORY 2 : _____

ACCESSORY 3 : _____

ACCESSORY 4 : _____

ACCESSORY 5 : _____

DISTANCE	1st TEST ( )	2nd TEST ( )	3rd TEST ( )	TOTAL ( )	AVERAGE ( )	ACCURACY (%)
1 M						
2 M						
3 M						
4 M						
5 M						
6 M						
7 M						
8 M						
9 M						
10 M						
____ M						
____ M						

NOTE : _____

_____

BLASTER : _____

TARGET : _____

TECHNIQUE : _____

_____

BULLET : _____

ACCESSORY 1 : _____

ACCESSORY 2 : _____

ACCESSORY 3 : _____

ACCESSORY 4 : _____

ACCESSORY 5 : _____

DISTANCE	1st TEST ( )	2nd TEST ( )	3rd TEST ( )	TOTAL ( )	AVERAGE ( )	ACCURACY (%)
1 M						
2 M						
3 M						
4 M						
5 M						
6 M						
7 M						
8 M						
9 M						
10 M						
_____ M						
_____ M						

NOTE : _____

_____

BLASTER : _____

TARGET : _____

TECHNIQUE : _____

_____

BULLET : _____

ACCESSORY 1 : _____

ACCESSORY 2 : _____

ACCESSORY 3 : _____

ACCESSORY 4 : _____

ACCESSORY 5 : _____

DISTANCE	1st TEST ( )	2nd TEST ( )	3rd TEST ( )	TOTAL ( )	AVERAGE ( )	ACCURACY (%)
1 M						
2 M						
3 M						
4 M						
5 M						
6 M						
7 M						
8 M						
9 M						
10 M						
___ M						
___ M						

NOTE : _____

_____

BLASTER : _____

TARGET : _____

TECHNIQUE : _____

_____

BULLET : _____

ACCESSORY 1 : _____

ACCESSORY 2 : _____

ACCESSORY 3 : _____

ACCESSORY 4 : _____

ACCESSORY 5 : _____

DISTANCE	1st TEST ( )	2nd TEST ( )	3rd TEST ( )	TOTAL ( )	AVERAGE ( )	ACCURACY (%)
1 M						
2 M						
3 M						
4 M						
5 M						
6 M						
7 M						
8 M						
9 M						
10 M						
_____ M						
_____ M						

NOTE : _____

_____

BLASTER : _____

TARGET : _____

TECHNIQUE : _____

_____

BULLET : _____

ACCESSORY 1 : _____

ACCESSORY 2 : _____

ACCESSORY 3 : _____

ACCESSORY 4 : _____

ACCESSORY 5 : _____

DISTANCE	1st TEST ( )	2nd TEST ( )	3rd TEST ( )	TOTAL ( )	AVERAGE ( )	ACCURACY (%)
1 M						
2 M						
3 M						
4 M						
5 M						
6 M						
7 M						
8 M						
9 M						
10 M						
___ M						
___ M						

NOTE : _____

_____

BLASTER : _____

TARGET : _____

TECHNIQUE : _____
_____

BULLET : _____

ACCESSORY 1 : _____

ACCESSORY 2 : _____

ACCESSORY 3 : _____

ACCESSORY 4 : _____

ACCESSORY 5 : _____

DISTANCE	1st TEST ( )	2nd TEST ( )	3rd TEST ( )	TOTAL ( )	AVERAGE ( )	ACCURACY (%)
1 M						
2 M						
3 M						
4 M						
5 M						
6 M						
7 M						
8 M						
9 M						
10 M						
_____ M						
_____ M						

NOTE : _____
_____

BLASTER : _____

TARGET : _____

TECHNIQUE : _____

_____

BULLET : _____

ACCESSORY 1 : _____

ACCESSORY 2 : _____

ACCESSORY 3 : _____

ACCESSORY 4 : _____

ACCESSORY 5 : _____

DISTANCE	1st TEST ( )	2nd TEST ( )	3rd TEST ( )	TOTAL ( )	AVERAGE ( )	ACCURACY (%)
1 M						
2 M						
3 M						
4 M						
5 M						
6 M						
7 M						
8 M						
9 M						
10 M						
____ M						
____ M						

NOTE : _____

_____

BLASTER : _____

TARGET : _____

TECHNIQUE : _____

_____

BULLET : _____

ACCESSORY 1 : _____

ACCESSORY 2 : _____

ACCESSORY 3 : _____

ACCESSORY 4 : _____

ACCESSORY 5 : _____

DISTANCE	1st TEST ( )	2nd TEST ( )	3rd TEST ( )	TOTAL ( )	AVERAGE ( )	ACCURACY (%)
1 M						
2 M						
3 M						
4 M						
5 M						
6 M						
7 M						
8 M						
9 M						
10 M						
_____ M						
_____ M						

NOTE : _____

_____

BLASTER : _____

TARGET : _____

TECHNIQUE : _____

_____

BULLET : _____

ACCESSORY 1 : _____

ACCESSORY 2 : _____

ACCESSORY 3 : _____

ACCESSORY 4 : _____

ACCESSORY 5 : _____

DISTANCE	1st TEST ( )	2nd TEST ( )	3rd TEST ( )	TOTAL ( )	AVERAGE ( )	ACCURACY (%)
1 M						
2 M						
3 M						
4 M						
5 M						
6 M						
7 M						
8 M						
9 M						
10 M						
____ M						
____ M						

NOTE : _____

_____

BLASTER : _____

TARGET : _____

TECHNIQUE : _____

_____

BULLET : _____

ACCESSORY 1 : _____

ACCESSORY 2 : _____

ACCESSORY 3 : _____

ACCESSORY 4 : _____

ACCESSORY 5 : _____

DISTANCE	1st TEST ( )	2nd TEST ( )	3rd TEST ( )	TOTAL ( )	AVERAGE ( )	ACCURACY (%)
1 M						
2 M						
3 M						
4 M						
5 M						
6 M						
7 M						
8 M						
9 M						
10 M						
____ M						
____ M						

NOTE : _____

_____

BLASTER : _____

TARGET : _____

TECHNIQUE : _____

_____

BULLET : _____

ACCESSORY 1 : _____

ACCESSORY 2 : _____

ACCESSORY 3 : _____

ACCESSORY 4 : _____

ACCESSORY 5 : _____

DISTANCE	1st TEST ( )	2nd TEST ( )	3rd TEST ( )	TOTAL ( )	AVERAGE ( )	ACCURACY (%)
1 M						
2 M						
3 M						
4 M						
5 M						
6 M						
7 M						
8 M						
9 M						
10 M						
___ M						
___ M						

NOTE : _____

_____

BLASTER : _____

TARGET : _____

TECHNIQUE : _____

_____

BULLET : _____

ACCESSORY 1 : _____

ACCESSORY 2 : _____

ACCESSORY 3 : _____

ACCESSORY 4 : _____

ACCESSORY 5 : _____

DISTANCE	1st TEST ( )	2nd TEST ( )	3rd TEST ( )	TOTAL ( )	AVERAGE ( )	ACCURACY (%)
1 M						
2 M						
3 M						
4 M						
5 M						
6 M						
7 M						
8 M						
9 M						
10 M						
_____ M						
_____ M						

NOTE : _____

_____

BLASTER : _____

TARGET : _____

TECHNIQUE : _____

_____

BULLET : _____

ACCESSORY 1 : _____

ACCESSORY 2 : _____

ACCESSORY 3 : _____

ACCESSORY 4 : _____

ACCESSORY 5 : _____

DISTANCE	1st TEST ( )	2nd TEST ( )	3rd TEST ( )	TOTAL ( )	AVERAGE ( )	ACCURACY (%)
1 M						
2 M						
3 M						
4 M						
5 M						
6 M						
7 M						
8 M						
9 M						
10 M						
____ M						
____ M						

NOTE : _____

_____

BLASTER : _____

TARGET : _____

TECHNIQUE : _____

_____

BULLET : _____

ACCESSORY 1 : _____

ACCESSORY 2 : _____

ACCESSORY 3 : _____

ACCESSORY 4 : _____

ACCESSORY 5 : _____

DISTANCE	1st TEST ( )	2nd TEST ( )	3rd TEST ( )	TOTAL ( )	AVERAGE ( )	ACCURACY (%)
1 M						
2 M						
3 M						
4 M						
5 M						
6 M						
7 M						
8 M						
9 M						
10 M						
____ M						
____ M						

NOTE : _____

_____

BLASTER : _____

TARGET : _____

TECHNIQUE : _____

_____

BULLET : _____

ACCESSORY 1 : _____

ACCESSORY 2 : _____

ACCESSORY 3 : _____

ACCESSORY 4 : _____

ACCESSORY 5 : _____

DISTANCE	1st TEST ( )	2nd TEST ( )	3rd TEST ( )	TOTAL ( )	AVERAGE ( )	ACCURACY (%)
1 M						
2 M						
3 M						
4 M						
5 M						
6 M						
7 M						
8 M						
9 M						
10 M						
____ M						
____ M						

NOTE : _____

_____

BLASTER : _____

TARGET : _____

TECHNIQUE : _____

_____

BULLET : _____

ACCESSORY 1 : _____

ACCESSORY 2 : _____

ACCESSORY 3 : _____

ACCESSORY 4 : _____

ACCESSORY 5 : _____

DISTANCE	1st TEST ( )	2nd TEST ( )	3rd TEST ( )	TOTAL ( )	AVERAGE ( )	ACCURACY (%)
1 M						
2 M						
3 M						
4 M						
5 M						
6 M						
7 M						
8 M						
9 M						
10 M						
____ M						
____ M						

NOTE : _____

_____

BLASTER : _____

TARGET : _____

TECHNIQUE : _____

_____

BULLET : _____

ACCESSORY 1 : _____

ACCESSORY 2 : _____

ACCESSORY 3 : _____

ACCESSORY 4 : _____

ACCESSORY 5 : _____

DISTANCE	1st TEST ( )	2nd TEST ( )	3rd TEST ( )	TOTAL ( )	AVERAGE ( )	ACCURACY (%)
1 M						
2 M						
3 M						
4 M						
5 M						
6 M						
7 M						
8 M						
9 M						
10 M						
___ M						
___ M						

NOTE : _____

_____

BLASTER : _____

TARGET : _____

TECHNIQUE : _____

_____

BULLET : _____

ACCESSORY 1 : _____

ACCESSORY 2 : _____

ACCESSORY 3 : _____

ACCESSORY 4 : _____

ACCESSORY 5 : _____

DISTANCE	1st TEST ( )	2nd TEST ( )	3rd TEST ( )	TOTAL ( )	AVERAGE ( )	ACCURACY (%)
1 M						
2 M						
3 M						
4 M						
5 M						
6 M						
7 M						
8 M						
9 M						
10 M						
_____ M						
_____ M						

NOTE : _____

_____

BLASTER : _____

TARGET : _____

TECHNIQUE : _____

_____

BULLET : _____

ACCESSORY 1 : _____

ACCESSORY 2 : _____

ACCESSORY 3 : _____

ACCESSORY 4 : _____

ACCESSORY 5 : _____

DISTANCE	1st TEST ( )	2nd TEST ( )	3rd TEST ( )	TOTAL ( )	AVERAGE ( )	ACCURACY (%)
1 M						
2 M						
3 M						
4 M						
5 M						
6 M						
7 M						
8 M						
9 M						
10 M						
____ M						
____ M						

NOTE : _____

_____

BLASTER : _____

TARGET : _____

TECHNIQUE : _____

_____

BULLET : _____

ACCESSORY 1 : _____

ACCESSORY 2 : _____

ACCESSORY 3 : _____

ACCESSORY 4 : _____

ACCESSORY 5 : _____

DISTANCE	1st TEST ( )	2nd TEST ( )	3rd TEST ( )	TOTAL ( )	AVERAGE ( )	ACCURACY (%)
1 M						
2 M						
3 M						
4 M						
5 M						
6 M						
7 M						
8 M						
9 M						
10 M						
____ M						
____ M						

NOTE : _____

_____

BLASTER : _____

TARGET : _____

TECHNIQUE : _____

_____

BULLET : _____

ACCESSORY 1 : _____

ACCESSORY 2 : _____

ACCESSORY 3 : _____

ACCESSORY 4 : _____

ACCESSORY 5 : _____

DISTANCE	1st TEST ( )	2nd TEST ( )	3rd TEST ( )	TOTAL ( )	AVERAGE ( )	ACCURACY (%)
1 M						
2 M						
3 M						
4 M						
5 M						
6 M						
7 M						
8 M						
9 M						
10 M						
____ M						
____ M						

NOTE : _____

_____

BLASTER : _____

TARGET : _____

TECHNIQUE : _____

_____

BULLET : _____

ACCESSORY 1 : _____

ACCESSORY 2 : _____

ACCESSORY 3 : _____

ACCESSORY 4 : _____

ACCESSORY 5 : _____

DISTANCE	1st TEST ( )	2nd TEST ( )	3rd TEST ( )	TOTAL ( )	AVERAGE ( )	ACCURACY (%)
1 M						
2 M						
3 M						
4 M						
5 M						
6 M						
7 M						
8 M						
9 M						
10 M						
_____ M						
_____ M						

NOTE : _____

_____

BLASTER : _____

TARGET : _____

TECHNIQUE : _____

_____

BULLET : _____

ACCESSORY 1 : _____

ACCESSORY 2 : _____

ACCESSORY 3 : _____

ACCESSORY 4 : _____

ACCESSORY 5 : _____

DISTANCE	1st TEST ( )	2nd TEST ( )	3rd TEST ( )	TOTAL ( )	AVERAGE ( )	ACCURACY (%)
1 M						
2 M						
3 M						
4 M						
5 M						
6 M						
7 M						
8 M						
9 M						
10 M						
____ M						
____ M						

NOTE : _____

_____

BLASTER : _____

TARGET : _____

TECHNIQUE : _____

_____

BULLET : _____

ACCESSORY 1 : _____

ACCESSORY 2 : _____

ACCESSORY 3 : _____

ACCESSORY 4 : _____

ACCESSORY 5 : _____

DISTANCE	1st TEST ( )	2nd TEST ( )	3rd TEST ( )	TOTAL ( )	AVERAGE ( )	ACCURACY (%)
1 M						
2 M						
3 M						
4 M						
5 M						
6 M						
7 M						
8 M						
9 M						
10 M						
_____ M						
_____ M						

NOTE : _____

_____

BLASTER : _____

TARGET : _____

TECHNIQUE : _____

_____

BULLET : _____

ACCESSORY 1 : _____

ACCESSORY 2 : _____

ACCESSORY 3 : _____

ACCESSORY 4 : _____

ACCESSORY 5 : _____

DISTANCE	1st TEST ( )	2nd TEST ( )	3rd TEST ( )	TOTAL ( )	AVERAGE ( )	ACCURACY (%)
1 M						
2 M						
3 M						
4 M						
5 M						
6 M						
7 M						
8 M						
9 M						
10 M						
___ M						
___ M						

NOTE : _____

_____

BLASTER : _____

TARGET : _____

TECHNIQUE : _____

_____

BULLET : _____

ACCESSORY 1 : _____

ACCESSORY 2 : _____

ACCESSORY 3 : _____

ACCESSORY 4 : _____

ACCESSORY 5 : _____

DISTANCE	1st TEST ( )	2nd TEST ( )	3rd TEST ( )	TOTAL ( )	AVERAGE ( )	ACCURACY (%)
1 M						
2 M						
3 M						
4 M						
5 M						
6 M						
7 M						
8 M						
9 M						
10 M						
____ M						
____ M						

NOTE : _____

_____

BLASTER : _____

TARGET : _____

TECHNIQUE : _____

_____

BULLET : _____

ACCESSORY 1 : _____

ACCESSORY 2 : _____

ACCESSORY 3 : _____

ACCESSORY 4 : _____

ACCESSORY 5 : _____

DISTANCE	1st TEST ( )	2nd TEST ( )	3rd TEST ( )	TOTAL ( )	AVERAGE ( )	ACCURACY (%)
1 M						
2 M						
3 M						
4 M						
5 M						
6 M						
7 M						
8 M						
9 M						
10 M						
____ M						
____ M						

NOTE : _____

_____

BLASTER : _____

TARGET : _____

TECHNIQUE : _____

_____

BULLET : _____

ACCESSORY 1 : _____

ACCESSORY 2 : _____

ACCESSORY 3 : _____

ACCESSORY 4 : _____

ACCESSORY 5 : _____

DISTANCE	1st TEST ( )	2nd TEST ( )	3rd TEST ( )	TOTAL ( )	AVERAGE ( )	ACCURACY (%)
1 M						
2 M						
3 M						
4 M						
5 M						
6 M						
7 M						
8 M						
9 M						
10 M						
____ M						
____ M						

NOTE : _____

_____

BLASTER : _____

TARGET : _____

TECHNIQUE : _____

_____

BULLET : _____

ACCESSORY 1 : _____

ACCESSORY 2 : _____

ACCESSORY 3 : _____

ACCESSORY 4 : _____

ACCESSORY 5 : _____

DISTANCE	1st TEST ( )	2nd TEST ( )	3rd TEST ( )	TOTAL ( )	AVERAGE ( )	ACCURACY (%)
1 M						
2 M						
3 M						
4 M						
5 M						
6 M						
7 M						
8 M						
9 M						
10 M						
_____ M						
_____ M						

NOTE : _____

_____

BLASTER : _____

TARGET : _____

TECHNIQUE : _____

_____

BULLET : _____

ACCESSORY 1 : _____

ACCESSORY 2 : _____

ACCESSORY 3 : _____

ACCESSORY 4 : _____

ACCESSORY 5 : _____

DISTANCE	1st TEST ( )	2nd TEST ( )	3rd TEST ( )	TOTAL ( )	AVERAGE ( )	ACCURACY (%)
1 M						
2 M						
3 M						
4 M						
5 M						
6 M						
7 M						
8 M						
9 M						
10 M						
_____ M						
_____ M						

NOTE : _____

_____

BLASTER : _____

TARGET : _____

TECHNIQUE : _____

_____

BULLET : _____

ACCESSORY 1 : _____

ACCESSORY 2 : _____

ACCESSORY 3 : _____

ACCESSORY 4 : _____

ACCESSORY 5 : _____

DISTANCE	1st TEST ( )	2nd TEST ( )	3rd TEST ( )	TOTAL ( )	AVERAGE ( )	ACCURACY (%)
1 M						
2 M						
3 M						
4 M						
5 M						
6 M						
7 M						
8 M						
9 M						
10 M						
____ M						
____ M						

NOTE : _____

_____

BLASTER : _____

TARGET : _____

TECHNIQUE : _____

_____

BULLET : _____

ACCESSORY 1 : _____

ACCESSORY 2 : _____

ACCESSORY 3 : _____

ACCESSORY 4 : _____

ACCESSORY 5 : _____

DISTANCE	1st TEST ( )	2nd TEST ( )	3rd TEST ( )	TOTAL ( )	AVERAGE ( )	ACCURACY (%)
1 M						
2 M						
3 M						
4 M						
5 M						
6 M						
7 M						
8 M						
9 M						
10 M						
_____ M						
_____ M						

NOTE : _____

_____

BLASTER : _____

TARGET : _____

TECHNIQUE : _____

_____

BULLET : _____

ACCESSORY 1 : _____

ACCESSORY 2 : _____

ACCESSORY 3 : _____

ACCESSORY 4 : _____

ACCESSORY 5 : _____

DISTANCE	1st TEST ( )	2nd TEST ( )	3rd TEST ( )	TOTAL ( )	AVERAGE ( )	ACCURACY (%)
1 M						
2 M						
3 M						
4 M						
5 M						
6 M						
7 M						
8 M						
9 M						
10 M						
____ M						
____ M						

NOTE : _____

_____

BLASTER : _____

TARGET : _____

TECHNIQUE : _____

_____

BULLET : _____

ACCESSORY 1 : _____

ACCESSORY 2 : _____

ACCESSORY 3 : _____

ACCESSORY 4 : _____

ACCESSORY 5 : _____

DISTANCE	1st TEST ( )	2nd TEST ( )	3rd TEST ( )	TOTAL ( )	AVERAGE ( )	ACCURACY (%)
1 M						
2 M						
3 M						
4 M						
5 M						
6 M						
7 M						
8 M						
9 M						
10 M						
_____ M						
_____ M						

NOTE : _____

_____

BLASTER : _____

TARGET : _____

TECHNIQUE : _____

_____

BULLET : _____

ACCESSORY 1 : _____

ACCESSORY 2 : _____

ACCESSORY 3 : _____

ACCESSORY 4 : _____

ACCESSORY 5 : _____

DISTANCE	1st TEST ( )	2nd TEST ( )	3rd TEST ( )	TOTAL ( )	AVERAGE ( )	ACCURACY (%)
1 M						
2 M						
3 M						
4 M						
5 M						
6 M						
7 M						
8 M						
9 M						
10 M						
____ M						
____ M						

NOTE : _____

_____

BLASTER : _____

TARGET : _____

TECHNIQUE : _____

_____

BULLET : _____

ACCESSORY 1 : _____

ACCESSORY 2 : _____

ACCESSORY 3 : _____

ACCESSORY 4 : _____

ACCESSORY 5 : _____

DISTANCE	1st TEST ( )	2nd TEST ( )	3rd TEST ( )	TOTAL ( )	AVERAGE ( )	ACCURACY (%)
1 M						
2 M						
3 M						
4 M						
5 M						
6 M						
7 M						
8 M						
9 M						
10 M						
_____ M						
_____ M						

NOTE : _____

_____

BLASTER : _____

TARGET : _____

TECHNIQUE : _____

_____

BULLET : _____

ACCESSORY 1 : _____

ACCESSORY 2 : _____

ACCESSORY 3 : _____

ACCESSORY 4 : _____

ACCESSORY 5 : _____

DISTANCE	1st TEST ( )	2nd TEST ( )	3rd TEST ( )	TOTAL ( )	AVERAGE ( )	ACCURACY (%)
1 M						
2 M						
3 M						
4 M						
5 M						
6 M						
7 M						
8 M						
9 M						
10 M						
____ M						
____ M						

NOTE : _____

_____

BLASTER : _____

TARGET : _____

TECHNIQUE : _____

_____

BULLET : _____

ACCESSORY 1 : _____

ACCESSORY 2 : _____

ACCESSORY 3 : _____

ACCESSORY 4 : _____

ACCESSORY 5 : _____

DISTANCE	1st TEST ( )	2nd TEST ( )	3rd TEST ( )	TOTAL ( )	AVERAGE ( )	ACCURACY (%)
1 M						
2 M						
3 M						
4 M						
5 M						
6 M						
7 M						
8 M						
9 M						
10 M						
_____ M						
_____ M						

NOTE : _____

_____

BLASTER : _____

TARGET : _____

TECHNIQUE : _____

_____

BULLET : _____

ACCESSORY 1 : _____

ACCESSORY 2 : _____

ACCESSORY 3 : _____

ACCESSORY 4 : _____

ACCESSORY 5 : _____

DISTANCE	1st TEST ( )	2nd TEST ( )	3rd TEST ( )	TOTAL ( )	AVERAGE ( )	ACCURACY (%)
1 M						
2 M						
3 M						
4 M						
5 M						
6 M						
7 M						
8 M						
9 M						
10 M						
____ M						
____ M						

NOTE : _____

_____

BLASTER : _____

TARGET : _____

TECHNIQUE : _____

_____

BULLET : _____

ACCESSORY 1 : _____

ACCESSORY 2 : _____

ACCESSORY 3 : _____

ACCESSORY 4 : _____

ACCESSORY 5 : _____

DISTANCE	1st TEST ( )	2nd TEST ( )	3rd TEST ( )	TOTAL ( )	AVERAGE ( )	ACCURACY (%)
1 M						
2 M						
3 M						
4 M						
5 M						
6 M						
7 M						
8 M						
9 M						
10 M						
_____ M						
_____ M						

NOTE : _____

_____

BLASTER : _____

TARGET : _____

TECHNIQUE : _____

_____

BULLET : _____

ACCESSORY 1 : _____

ACCESSORY 2 : _____

ACCESSORY 3 : _____

ACCESSORY 4 : _____

ACCESSORY 5 : _____

DISTANCE	1st TEST ( )	2nd TEST ( )	3rd TEST ( )	TOTAL ( )	AVERAGE ( )	ACCURACY (%)
1 M						
2 M						
3 M						
4 M						
5 M						
6 M						
7 M						
8 M						
9 M						
10 M						
____ M						
____ M						

NOTE : _____

_____

BLASTER : _____

TARGET : _____

TECHNIQUE : _____

_____

BULLET : _____

ACCESSORY 1 : _____

ACCESSORY 2 : _____

ACCESSORY 3 : _____

ACCESSORY 4 : _____

ACCESSORY 5 : _____

DISTANCE	1st TEST ( )	2nd TEST ( )	3rd TEST ( )	TOTAL ( )	AVERAGE ( )	ACCURACY (%)
1 M						
2 M						
3 M						
4 M						
5 M						
6 M						
7 M						
8 M						
9 M						
10 M						
___ M						
___ M						

NOTE : _____

_____

BLASTER : _____

TARGET : _____

TECHNIQUE : _____

_____

BULLET : _____

ACCESSORY 1 : _____

ACCESSORY 2 : _____

ACCESSORY 3 : _____

ACCESSORY 4 : _____

ACCESSORY 5 : _____

DISTANCE	1st TEST ( )	2nd TEST ( )	3rd TEST ( )	TOTAL ( )	AVERAGE ( )	ACCURACY (%)
1 M						
2 M						
3 M						
4 M						
5 M						
6 M						
7 M						
8 M						
9 M						
10 M						
_____ M						
_____ M						

NOTE : _____

_____

BLASTER : _____

TARGET : _____

TECHNIQUE : _____

_____

BULLET : _____

ACCESSORY 1 : _____

ACCESSORY 2 : _____

ACCESSORY 3 : _____

ACCESSORY 4 : _____

ACCESSORY 5 : _____

DISTANCE	1st TEST ( )	2nd TEST ( )	3rd TEST ( )	TOTAL ( )	AVERAGE ( )	ACCURACY (%)
1 M						
2 M						
3 M						
4 M						
5 M						
6 M						
7 M						
8 M						
9 M						
10 M						
_____ M						
_____ M						

NOTE : _____

_____

BLASTER : _____

TARGET : _____

TECHNIQUE : _____

_____

BULLET : _____

ACCESSORY 1 : _____

ACCESSORY 2 : _____

ACCESSORY 3 : _____

ACCESSORY 4 : _____

ACCESSORY 5 : _____

DISTANCE	1st TEST ( )	2nd TEST ( )	3rd TEST ( )	TOTAL ( )	AVERAGE ( )	ACCURACY (%)
1 M						
2 M						
3 M						
4 M						
5 M						
6 M						
7 M						
8 M						
9 M						
10 M						
___ M						
___ M						

NOTE : _____

_____

BLASTER : _____

TARGET : _____

TECHNIQUE : _____

_____

BULLET : _____

ACCESSORY 1 : _____

ACCESSORY 2 : _____

ACCESSORY 3 : _____

ACCESSORY 4 : _____

ACCESSORY 5 : _____

DISTANCE	1st TEST ( )	2nd TEST ( )	3rd TEST ( )	TOTAL ( )	AVERAGE ( )	ACCURACY (%)
1 M						
2 M						
3 M						
4 M						
5 M						
6 M						
7 M						
8 M						
9 M						
10 M						
_____ M						
_____ M						

NOTE : _____

_____

BLASTER : _____

TARGET : _____

TECHNIQUE : _____

_____

BULLET : _____

ACCESSORY 1 : _____

ACCESSORY 2 : _____

ACCESSORY 3 : _____

ACCESSORY 4 : _____

ACCESSORY 5 : _____

DISTANCE	1st TEST ( )	2nd TEST ( )	3rd TEST ( )	TOTAL ( )	AVERAGE ( )	ACCURACY (%)
1 M						
2 M						
3 M						
4 M						
5 M						
6 M						
7 M						
8 M						
9 M						
10 M						
___ M						
___ M						

NOTE : _____

_____

BLASTER : _____

TARGET : _____

TECHNIQUE : _____

_____

BULLET : _____

ACCESSORY 1 : _____

ACCESSORY 2 : _____

ACCESSORY 3 : _____

ACCESSORY 4 : _____

ACCESSORY 5 : _____

DISTANCE	1st TEST ( )	2nd TEST ( )	3rd TEST ( )	TOTAL ( )	AVERAGE ( )	ACCURACY (%)
1 M						
2 M						
3 M						
4 M						
5 M						
6 M						
7 M						
8 M						
9 M						
10 M						
_____ M						
_____ M						

NOTE : _____

_____

BLASTER : _____

TARGET : _____

TECHNIQUE : _____

_____

BULLET : _____

ACCESSORY 1 : _____

ACCESSORY 2 : _____

ACCESSORY 3 : _____

ACCESSORY 4 : _____

ACCESSORY 5 : _____

DISTANCE	1st TEST ( )	2nd TEST ( )	3rd TEST ( )	TOTAL ( )	AVERAGE ( )	ACCURACY (%)
1 M						
2 M						
3 M						
4 M						
5 M						
6 M						
7 M						
8 M						
9 M						
10 M						
_____ M						
_____ M						

NOTE : _____

_____

BLASTER : _____

TARGET : _____

TECHNIQUE : _____

_____

BULLET : _____

ACCESSORY 1 : _____

ACCESSORY 2 : _____

ACCESSORY 3 : _____

ACCESSORY 4 : _____

ACCESSORY 5 : _____

DISTANCE	1st TEST ( )	2nd TEST ( )	3rd TEST ( )	TOTAL ( )	AVERAGE ( )	ACCURACY (%)
1 M						
2 M						
3 M						
4 M						
5 M						
6 M						
7 M						
8 M						
9 M						
10 M						
_____ M						
_____ M						

NOTE : _____

_____

BLASTER : _____

TARGET : _____

TECHNIQUE : _____

_____

BULLET : _____

ACCESSORY 1 : _____

ACCESSORY 2 : _____

ACCESSORY 3 : _____

ACCESSORY 4 : _____

ACCESSORY 5 : _____

DISTANCE	1st TEST ( )	2nd TEST ( )	3rd TEST ( )	TOTAL ( )	AVERAGE ( )	ACCURACY (%)
1 M						
2 M						
3 M						
4 M						
5 M						
6 M						
7 M						
8 M						
9 M						
10 M						
____ M						
____ M						

NOTE : _____

_____

BLASTER : _____

TARGET : _____

TECHNIQUE : _____

_____

BULLET : _____

ACCESSORY 1 : _____

ACCESSORY 2 : _____

ACCESSORY 3 : _____

ACCESSORY 4 : _____

ACCESSORY 5 : _____

DISTANCE	1st TEST ( )	2nd TEST ( )	3rd TEST ( )	TOTAL ( )	AVERAGE ( )	ACCURACY (%)
1 M						
2 M						
3 M						
4 M						
5 M						
6 M						
7 M						
8 M						
9 M						
10 M						
_____ M						
_____ M						

NOTE : _____

_____

BLASTER : _____

TARGET : _____

TECHNIQUE : _____

_____

BULLET : _____

ACCESSORY 1 : _____

ACCESSORY 2 : _____

ACCESSORY 3 : _____

ACCESSORY 4 : _____

ACCESSORY 5 : _____

DISTANCE	1st TEST ( )	2nd TEST ( )	3rd TEST ( )	TOTAL ( )	AVERAGE ( )	ACCURACY (%)
1 M						
2 M						
3 M						
4 M						
5 M						
6 M						
7 M						
8 M						
9 M						
10 M						
____ M						
____ M						

NOTE : _____

_____

BLASTER : _____

TARGET : _____

TECHNIQUE : _____

_____

BULLET : _____

ACCESSORY 1 : _____

ACCESSORY 2 : _____

ACCESSORY 3 : _____

ACCESSORY 4 : _____

ACCESSORY 5 : _____

DISTANCE	1st TEST ( )	2nd TEST ( )	3rd TEST ( )	TOTAL ( )	AVERAGE ( )	ACCURACY (%)
1 M						
2 M						
3 M						
4 M						
5 M						
6 M						
7 M						
8 M						
9 M						
10 M						
_____ M						
_____ M						

NOTE : _____

_____

BLASTER : _____

TARGET : _____

TECHNIQUE : _____

_____

BULLET : _____

ACCESSORY 1 : _____

ACCESSORY 2 : _____

ACCESSORY 3 : _____

ACCESSORY 4 : _____

ACCESSORY 5 : _____

DISTANCE	1st TEST ( )	2nd TEST ( )	3rd TEST ( )	TOTAL ( )	AVERAGE ( )	ACCURACY (%)
1 M						
2 M						
3 M						
4 M						
5 M						
6 M						
7 M						
8 M						
9 M						
10 M						
____ M						
____ M						

NOTE : _____

_____

BLASTER : _____

TARGET : _____

TECHNIQUE : _____

_____

BULLET : _____

ACCESSORY 1 : _____

ACCESSORY 2 : _____

ACCESSORY 3 : _____

ACCESSORY 4 : _____

ACCESSORY 5 : _____

DISTANCE	1st TEST ( )	2nd TEST ( )	3rd TEST ( )	TOTAL ( )	AVERAGE ( )	ACCURACY (%)
1 M						
2 M						
3 M						
4 M						
5 M						
6 M						
7 M						
8 M						
9 M						
10 M						
___ M						
___ M						

NOTE : _____

_____

BLASTER : _____

TARGET : _____

TECHNIQUE : _____

_____

BULLET : _____

ACCESSORY 1 : _____

ACCESSORY 2 : _____

ACCESSORY 3 : _____

ACCESSORY 4 : _____

ACCESSORY 5 : _____

DISTANCE	1st TEST ( )	2nd TEST ( )	3rd TEST ( )	TOTAL ( )	AVERAGE ( )	ACCURACY (%)
1 M						
2 M						
3 M						
4 M						
5 M						
6 M						
7 M						
8 M						
9 M						
10 M						
____ M						
____ M						

NOTE : _____

_____

BLASTER : _____

TARGET : _____

TECHNIQUE : _____

_____

BULLET : _____

ACCESSORY 1 : _____

ACCESSORY 2 : _____

ACCESSORY 3 : _____

ACCESSORY 4 : _____

ACCESSORY 5 : _____

DISTANCE	1st TEST ( )	2nd TEST ( )	3rd TEST ( )	TOTAL ( )	AVERAGE ( )	ACCURACY (%)
1 M						
2 M						
3 M						
4 M						
5 M						
6 M						
7 M						
8 M						
9 M						
10 M						
____ M						
____ M						

NOTE : _____

_____

BLASTER : _____

TARGET : _____

TECHNIQUE : _____

_____

BULLET : _____

ACCESSORY 1 : _____

ACCESSORY 2 : _____

ACCESSORY 3 : _____

ACCESSORY 4 : _____

ACCESSORY 5 : _____

DISTANCE	1st TEST ( )	2nd TEST ( )	3rd TEST ( )	TOTAL ( )	AVERAGE ( )	ACCURACY (%)
1 M						
2 M						
3 M						
4 M						
5 M						
6 M						
7 M						
8 M						
9 M						
10 M						
____ M						
____ M						

NOTE : _____

_____

BLASTER : _____

TARGET : _____

TECHNIQUE : _____

_____

BULLET : _____

ACCESSORY 1 : _____

ACCESSORY 2 : _____

ACCESSORY 3 : _____

ACCESSORY 4 : _____

ACCESSORY 5 : _____

DISTANCE	1st TEST ( )	2nd TEST ( )	3rd TEST ( )	TOTAL ( )	AVERAGE ( )	ACCURACY (%)
1 M						
2 M						
3 M						
4 M						
5 M						
6 M						
7 M						
8 M						
9 M						
10 M						
_____ M						
_____ M						

NOTE : _____

_____

BLASTER : _____

TARGET : _____

TECHNIQUE : _____

_____

BULLET : _____

ACCESSORY 1 : _____

ACCESSORY 2 : _____

ACCESSORY 3 : _____

ACCESSORY 4 : _____

ACCESSORY 5 : _____

DISTANCE	1st TEST ( )	2nd TEST ( )	3rd TEST ( )	TOTAL ( )	AVERAGE ( )	ACCURACY (%)
1 M						
2 M						
3 M						
4 M						
5 M						
6 M						
7 M						
8 M						
9 M						
10 M						
____ M						
____ M						

NOTE : _____

_____

BLASTER : _____

TARGET : _____

TECHNIQUE : _____

_____

BULLET : _____

ACCESSORY 1 : _____

ACCESSORY 2 : _____

ACCESSORY 3 : _____

ACCESSORY 4 : _____

ACCESSORY 5 : _____

DISTANCE	1st TEST ( )	2nd TEST ( )	3rd TEST ( )	TOTAL ( )	AVERAGE ( )	ACCURACY (%)
1 M						
2 M						
3 M						
4 M						
5 M						
6 M						
7 M						
8 M						
9 M						
10 M						
____ M						
____ M						

NOTE : _____

_____

BLASTER : _____

TARGET : _____

TECHNIQUE : _____

_____

BULLET : _____

ACCESSORY 1 : _____

ACCESSORY 2 : _____

ACCESSORY 3 : _____

ACCESSORY 4 : _____

ACCESSORY 5 : _____

DISTANCE	1st TEST ( )	2nd TEST ( )	3rd TEST ( )	TOTAL ( )	AVERAGE ( )	ACCURACY (%)
1 M						
2 M						
3 M						
4 M						
5 M						
6 M						
7 M						
8 M						
9 M						
10 M						
____M						
____M						

NOTE : _____

_____

BLASTER : _____

TARGET : _____

TECHNIQUE : _____

_____

BULLET : _____

ACCESSORY 1 : _____

ACCESSORY 2 : _____

ACCESSORY 3 : _____

ACCESSORY 4 : _____

ACCESSORY 5 : _____

DISTANCE	1st TEST ( )	2nd TEST ( )	3rd TEST ( )	TOTAL ( )	AVERAGE ( )	ACCURACY (%)
1 M						
2 M						
3 M						
4 M						
5 M						
6 M						
7 M						
8 M						
9 M						
10 M						
___ M						
___ M						

NOTE : _____

_____

BLASTER : _____

TARGET : _____

TECHNIQUE : _____

_____

BULLET : _____

ACCESSORY 1 : _____

ACCESSORY 2 : _____

ACCESSORY 3 : _____

ACCESSORY 4 : _____

ACCESSORY 5 : _____

DISTANCE	1st TEST ( )	2nd TEST ( )	3rd TEST ( )	TOTAL ( )	AVERAGE ( )	ACCURACY (%)
1 M						
2 M						
3 M						
4 M						
5 M						
6 M						
7 M						
8 M						
9 M						
10 M						
____ M						
____ M						

NOTE : _____

_____

BLASTER : _____

TARGET : _____

TECHNIQUE : _____

_____

BULLET : _____

ACCESSORY 1 : _____

ACCESSORY 2 : _____

ACCESSORY 3 : _____

ACCESSORY 4 : _____

ACCESSORY 5 : _____

DISTANCE	1st TEST ( )	2nd TEST ( )	3rd TEST ( )	TOTAL ( )	AVERAGE ( )	ACCURACY (%)
1 M						
2 M						
3 M						
4 M						
5 M						
6 M						
7 M						
8 M						
9 M						
10 M						
___ M						
___ M						

NOTE : _____

_____

BLASTER : _____

TARGET : _____

TECHNIQUE : _____

_____

BULLET : _____

ACCESSORY 1 : _____

ACCESSORY 2 : _____

ACCESSORY 3 : _____

ACCESSORY 4 : _____

ACCESSORY 5 : _____

DISTANCE	1st TEST ( )	2nd TEST ( )	3rd TEST ( )	TOTAL ( )	AVERAGE ( )	ACCURACY (%)
1 M						
2 M						
3 M						
4 M						
5 M						
6 M						
7 M						
8 M						
9 M						
10 M						
____ M						
____ M						

NOTE : _____

_____

BLASTER : _____

TARGET : _____

TECHNIQUE : _____

_____

BULLET : _____

ACCESSORY 1 : _____

ACCESSORY 2 : _____

ACCESSORY 3 : _____

ACCESSORY 4 : _____

ACCESSORY 5 : _____

DISTANCE	1st TEST ( )	2nd TEST ( )	3rd TEST ( )	TOTAL ( )	AVERAGE ( )	ACCURACY (%)
1 M						
2 M						
3 M						
4 M						
5 M						
6 M						
7 M						
8 M						
9 M						
10 M						
____ M						
____ M						

NOTE : _____

_____

BLASTER : _____

TARGET : _____

TECHNIQUE : _____

_____

BULLET : _____

ACCESSORY 1 : _____

ACCESSORY 2 : _____

ACCESSORY 3 : _____

ACCESSORY 4 : _____

ACCESSORY 5 : _____

DISTANCE	1st TEST ( )	2nd TEST ( )	3rd TEST ( )	TOTAL ( )	AVERAGE ( )	ACCURACY (%)
1 M						
2 M						
3 M						
4 M						
5 M						
6 M						
7 M						
8 M						
9 M						
10 M						
____ M						
____ M						

NOTE : _____

_____

BLASTER : _____

TARGET : _____

TECHNIQUE : _____

_____

BULLET : _____

ACCESSORY 1 : _____

ACCESSORY 2 : _____

ACCESSORY 3 : _____

ACCESSORY 4 : _____

ACCESSORY 5 : _____

DISTANCE	1st TEST ( )	2nd TEST ( )	3rd TEST ( )	TOTAL ( )	AVERAGE ( )	ACCURACY (%)
1 M						
2 M						
3 M						
4 M						
5 M						
6 M						
7 M						
8 M						
9 M						
10 M						
____ M						
____ M						

NOTE : _____

_____

BLASTER : _____

TARGET : _____

TECHNIQUE : _____

_____

BULLET : _____

ACCESSORY 1 : _____

ACCESSORY 2 : _____

ACCESSORY 3 : _____

ACCESSORY 4 : _____

ACCESSORY 5 : _____

DISTANCE	1st TEST ( )	2nd TEST ( )	3rd TEST ( )	TOTAL ( )	AVERAGE ( )	ACCURACY (%)
1 M						
2 M						
3 M						
4 M						
5 M						
6 M						
7 M						
8 M						
9 M						
10 M						
____ M						
____ M						

NOTE : _____

_____

BLASTER : _____

TARGET : _____

TECHNIQUE : _____

_____

BULLET : _____

ACCESSORY 1 : _____

ACCESSORY 2 : _____

ACCESSORY 3 : _____

ACCESSORY 4 : _____

ACCESSORY 5 : _____

DISTANCE	1st TEST ( )	2nd TEST ( )	3rd TEST ( )	TOTAL ( )	AVERAGE ( )	ACCURACY (%)
1 M						
2 M						
3 M						
4 M						
5 M						
6 M						
7 M						
8 M						
9 M						
10 M						
_____ M						
_____ M						

NOTE : _____

_____

BLASTER : _____

TARGET : _____

TECHNIQUE : _____

_____

BULLET : _____

ACCESSORY 1 : _____

ACCESSORY 2 : _____

ACCESSORY 3 : _____

ACCESSORY 4 : _____

ACCESSORY 5 : _____

DISTANCE	1st TEST ( )	2nd TEST ( )	3rd TEST ( )	TOTAL ( )	AVERAGE ( )	ACCURACY (%)
1 M						
2 M						
3 M						
4 M						
5 M						
6 M						
7 M						
8 M						
9 M						
10 M						
____ M						
____ M						

NOTE : _____

_____

BLASTER : _____

TARGET : _____

TECHNIQUE : _____

_____

BULLET : _____

ACCESSORY 1 : _____

ACCESSORY 2 : _____

ACCESSORY 3 : _____

ACCESSORY 4 : _____

ACCESSORY 5 : _____

DISTANCE	1st TEST ( )	2nd TEST ( )	3rd TEST ( )	TOTAL ( )	AVERAGE ( )	ACCURACY (%)
1 M						
2 M						
3 M						
4 M						
5 M						
6 M						
7 M						
8 M						
9 M						
10 M						
_____ M						
_____ M						

NOTE : _____

_____

BLASTER : _____

TARGET : _____

TECHNIQUE : _____

_____

BULLET : _____

ACCESSORY 1 : _____

ACCESSORY 2 : _____

ACCESSORY 3 : _____

ACCESSORY 4 : _____

ACCESSORY 5 : _____

DISTANCE	1st TEST ( )	2nd TEST ( )	3rd TEST ( )	TOTAL ( )	AVERAGE ( )	ACCURACY (%)
1 M						
2 M						
3 M						
4 M						
5 M						
6 M						
7 M						
8 M						
9 M						
10 M						
____ M						
____ M						

NOTE : _____

_____

BLASTER : _____

TARGET : _____

TECHNIQUE : _____

_____

BULLET : _____

ACCESSORY 1 : _____

ACCESSORY 2 : _____

ACCESSORY 3 : _____

ACCESSORY 4 : _____

ACCESSORY 5 : _____

DISTANCE	1st TEST ( )	2nd TEST ( )	3rd TEST ( )	TOTAL ( )	AVERAGE ( )	ACCURACY (%)
1 M						
2 M						
3 M						
4 M						
5 M						
6 M						
7 M						
8 M						
9 M						
10 M						
_____ M						
_____ M						

NOTE : _____

_____

BLASTER : _____

TARGET : _____

TECHNIQUE : _____

_____

BULLET : _____

ACCESSORY 1 : _____

ACCESSORY 2 : _____

ACCESSORY 3 : _____

ACCESSORY 4 : _____

ACCESSORY 5 : _____

DISTANCE	1st TEST ( )	2nd TEST ( )	3rd TEST ( )	TOTAL ( )	AVERAGE ( )	ACCURACY (%)
1 M						
2 M						
3 M						
4 M						
5 M						
6 M						
7 M						
8 M						
9 M						
10 M						
____ M						
____ M						

NOTE : _____

_____

BLASTER : _____

TARGET : _____

TECHNIQUE : _____

_____

BULLET : _____

ACCESSORY 1 : _____

ACCESSORY 2 : _____

ACCESSORY 3 : _____

ACCESSORY 4 : _____

ACCESSORY 5 : _____

DISTANCE	1st TEST ( )	2nd TEST ( )	3rd TEST ( )	TOTAL ( )	AVERAGE ( )	ACCURACY (%)
1 M						
2 M						
3 M						
4 M						
5 M						
6 M						
7 M						
8 M						
9 M						
10 M						
____ M						
____ M						

NOTE : _____

_____

BLASTER : _____

TARGET : _____

TECHNIQUE : _____

_____

BULLET : _____

ACCESSORY 1 : _____

ACCESSORY 2 : _____

ACCESSORY 3 : _____

ACCESSORY 4 : _____

ACCESSORY 5 : _____

DISTANCE	1st TEST ( )	2nd TEST ( )	3rd TEST ( )	TOTAL ( )	AVERAGE ( )	ACCURACY (%)
1 M						
2 M						
3 M						
4 M						
5 M						
6 M						
7 M						
8 M						
9 M						
10 M						
____ M						
____ M						

NOTE : _____

_____

BLASTER : _____

TARGET : _____

TECHNIQUE : _____

_____

BULLET : _____

ACCESSORY 1 : _____

ACCESSORY 2 : _____

ACCESSORY 3 : _____

ACCESSORY 4 : _____

ACCESSORY 5 : _____

DISTANCE	1st TEST ( )	2nd TEST ( )	3rd TEST ( )	TOTAL ( )	AVERAGE ( )	ACCURACY (%)
1 M						
2 M						
3 M						
4 M						
5 M						
6 M						
7 M						
8 M						
9 M						
10 M						
____ M						
____ M						

NOTE : _____

_____

BLASTER : _____

TARGET : _____

TECHNIQUE : _____

_____

BULLET : _____

ACCESSORY 1 : _____

ACCESSORY 2 : _____

ACCESSORY 3 : _____

ACCESSORY 4 : _____

ACCESSORY 5 : _____

DISTANCE	1st TEST ( )	2nd TEST ( )	3rd TEST ( )	TOTAL ( )	AVERAGE ( )	ACCURACY (%)
1 M						
2 M						
3 M						
4 M						
5 M						
6 M						
7 M						
8 M						
9 M						
10 M						
____ M						
____ M						

NOTE : _____

_____

BLASTER : _____

TARGET : _____

TECHNIQUE : _____

_____

BULLET : _____

ACCESSORY 1 : _____

ACCESSORY 2 : _____

ACCESSORY 3 : _____

ACCESSORY 4 : _____

ACCESSORY 5 : _____

DISTANCE	1st TEST ( )	2nd TEST ( )	3rd TEST ( )	TOTAL ( )	AVERAGE ( )	ACCURACY (%)
1 M						
2 M						
3 M						
4 M						
5 M						
6 M						
7 M						
8 M						
9 M						
10 M						
_____ M						
_____ M						

NOTE : _____

_____

NOTE

NOTE

NOTE

Made in the USA
Middletown, DE
28 November 2017